BLAKWORK

CU00802864

BLAKWORK

ALISON WHITTAKER

Magabala
Books

First published 2018, reprinted 2018 x2
Magabala Books Aboriginal Corporation
1 Bagot Street, Broome, Western Australia
Website: www.magabala.com
Email: sales@magabala.com

Magabala Books receives financial assistance from the Commonwealth Government through the
Australia Council, its arts advisory body. The State of Western Australia has made an investment
in this project through the Department of Local Government, Sport and Cultural Industries.
Magabala Books would like to acknowledge the generous support of the Shire of Broome,
Western Australia.

Copyright © Alison Whittaker, Text, 2018

The author asserts her moral rights.

All rights reserved. Apart from any fair dealing for the purposes of private study, research,
criticism or review, as permitted under the Copyright Act, no part of this publication may be
reproduced by any process whatsoever without the written permission of the publisher.

Cover Design Lijahdia Designs
Typeset by Post Pre-press Group
Printed and bound by Griffin Press, South Australia

 A catalogue record for this
book is available from the
National Library of Australia

'For your back'

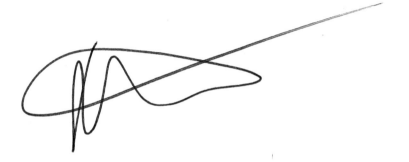

contents

whitework

BLAKWORK

Fresh blakwork; industrial complexes
hands with
smooth and flat palm callouses.

      Soothing re—
              —conciliation.

That dawdling off-trend meme,
white guilt. To survive among it; well,

      it's naff to say, but compul—

          —sory to do. Indentured blakwork, something like:

      nine to five, forgiv—
              —ing you.

not one silent lamb

1.

a tuft of sustenance, adrip with meat
and wool, pads the clay

2.

a hungry metaphor born, it breaches
somewhere out from Botany Bay

3.

smeared on a frontier ill-defined
beneath it bleats this grass-fed mine

4.

there is nothing less ill-
defined here. still them nullius men
carry that hard frontier, guard

these rhythmless feet

5.

a trespassing sheep.

a love like Dorothea's

I loved a sunburnt country, dislodged in a memory
I never lived in time to love a love like Dorothea's.
We're cannibals of other kinds; the white woman has eat the sky
and where's that leave them girls like I?—lost creatures chewing o'er the night

of our missing sunburnt country, on which our prone feet land.
Yet onto which Mackellar's gaze turns rivers into sand.

It burns my eyes to turn to hers, my wide brown land out of like hands
but traced in fetish verse—
'I love a sunburnt country'   I loved a sunburnt country.

                                        I love white nativity
that digs its roots and ticks to suck the floodplains and the sea—
the love that swept those sweeping plains from Nan, from Mum, from me.

Cored in my heart, my country—beauty, terror, balm and bite
building, taking flesh, building furnace, taking flight.

5

Lavish and demanding; driving lapping cattle off—while emu
and kang'roo alike on highway going soft.

I could have loved them twisting grass-fans—
grabbing motes with bubby hands—
like I loved this dutied vastness; that I am less and less than land.

I loved a sunburnt country—won't it
please come back to me? Won't it
show me why my spirit wanders
but is never free?
I will soothe its burns with lotion, I will peel off its dead skin.
If it can tell me
why I'm
drifting
ever further from my kin.
I loved a sunburnt country, won't it
gingerly limp back?
I can't get past the concrete and my blak tongue's gone all slack.

I'm sorry, sweet Mackellar, that it famished all your cows,
paddock's *yellow-thirsty-sudden-green*; no telling how.
That the *gold-hush-rainy-drum* was hard to violence and the plow.

I love a sunburnt country.   I love a sunburnt country.

I love a sunburnt country.
That is mine but not for me.

grapple gap

a   gap

overworked   under-reached
come   an'   pull   me   o'er the breach

warded of you   toward you skewed
live   another twenty years

if   I   live   them   —   like you'd.

goodblak

our pregnant vignette
endure transform triumph

endure
pure
authentic
sourcelessly

transform
outward
neutral
exhaustively

triumph
popular
proprietary
remorselessly

Anthropocene

If I am the roots
and you are the branches the
trunk and the leaves then

I will suck no deeper for
water

You leave here with me.

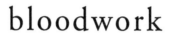

bloodwork

MANY GIRLS WHITE LINEN

no mist no mystery
no hanging rock only

many girls white linen
men with guns and
harsher things white women
amongst gums white linen
starch'er things later plaques
will mark this war
nails peeling back floor
scrubbing back blak chores
white luxe hangnails hanging
more than nails while
no palm glowing paler

later plaques will mark
this sick linen's rotten
cotton genes later plaques
will track the try
to bleed lineage dry

its banks now flood

a new ancestor, Ordeal,
plaits this our blood

if evil is banal
how more boring is
suffering evil two bloodlines
from it how more
raw rousing horrifying is
the plaque that marks
something else rolling on
from this place a
roll of white linen
dropped on slight incline
amongst gums collecting grit
where blak girls hang
nails hang out picking
them hangnails

COTTON ON

let's compare hands   s t r e t   c   h

tendons, wrists across   o c e   a   n   s

here: a common   wound.

heartwork

The vacuum ventricle's pitching hard; muscle heart
tough'ning, tough'ning, tough'ning
three yinarr I know gone out
one atrium at a time.

And them rhythms thrummed in lieu. Soft and blue—
I knew;   I knew—
from their bruised parts
we grew and grew, from
lips that coup, that teeth eschew
and rowdy tongues even words pursued.

Knew that breath on growing ear; steady and near, now hot with fear
that to yinarr's hearts work aims anew—colonially tired, colonially blue.

the grey saltbush

'Full-blooded?'

Your other fullness is round
and stretching—a belly
whose fullness was hellish.

We
and others speak your fullness sans sound.

'Full-blooded?'

Half of you's by the ground while

the other half's in books:
'The last hope, the last, the Machiavelli!'

Your fullness more than blood
and know no blood could make we women full.

So, it wove through us, resisting the flag
unscathed by its promise of our inevitable fade.

'The last?'

Did blak girls merely play

while all hope sank further still? No.
With panicked strength
fullness broke through like sapling life from the slag.

We mutt bastards grown
this fragile reserve 'round your legacy's length.

factor factory

in this poem we visit a safe house.

lungs of discount milk and
bones of torus-fractured women
a skin resisting theory like

trauma'ed men turn on
their ilk and double yinarr's
share? them men fill-in
colonial might
punch down, hope ground push up?

some say them trauma'ed
ones alike got culture push
ing down on them? or alco
hol or other drugs char
ge behind them right-
left-right slugs. or other eu
phemistic slurs 'bout sav
age women cowed in huts.

the torus women spin on spin sprout
seed weave refuge to the refuge house
mumbling the milk's run out.

bpm

100

Building, building, building blak
Our flesh fillin' up them gaps.

Ah, build love; so many blaks
How could I name them all?

Inner-city arty blak
Remote yet so connected blak
Welfare woman villain blak
Pension weaver striking blak
Work two jobs to make rent blak
Lawyer and professor blak
Third week on my couch now blak.

Women's fighter, healer blak
Deft protesting expert blak
Raiser, grower-upper blak
Anti-corporate commune blak
Lovin' up bank exec blak.

Compromised and trembling blak
Budding, getting thicker blak.

Meshed in the commun'ty blak
Only one in office blak.

Open blak, closet blak
Liminal and spongey blaks.

Football player hunky blak
Mermaid, bearded, chunky blak
Flaming blak, complaining blak
Got afro got a mullet blak.

Rooted in and by love blak
Two tids twined together blak
Brotha with anotha blak
With their chubby bubbies, blak
Budding and transforming blak
Tender gender made real blak.

Did I name the healing blak?

120

Baby in his belly blak
Baby on her shoulder blak

NGO stock photo blak
Juvenile bad mugshot blak
Alternative school photo blak

Poem from his sister blak
Tid with silent first name blak
All those loved and missed her blak
Gulping by a blank screen blak.

80

Heart is full and burstin' blak
Cynical in armchair blak

Skin like coolin' night sky black
Skin like earth in flight dust blak
Skin like firecourse now blak
Skin like glare off noon clouds blak
Skin like. Blak, skin like. Blak.

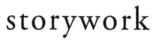

storywork

artwork

Its ancient work the machine rolls on.

A winding programme tells her hands
expertly where the fibres slip from
lands and for the lands, here land.

Her threads all line up, decades long
continue, fray, and touch but briefly.

Her fingers mottle.
The rope is made.

By which time she's greyed and griefly.

Its ancient work the machine rolls on
mob macramé, splicing cord.

Sealing fire lick-chase its end—
a plywood ten-buck boomerang.

stock image

Stock image barefoot child
Dirt path plait with tyre tracks
Full belly, propped tongue, chicken legs.

Kid with pea-thick flies on face
Thumbnail tucked into the teeth
Eyelids, mouth, dust membrane dregs.

A parent with bub locked to hip
Gaze on the lens, bub looking up
Left arm dangles, toes dug, heels ready.

High-vis wearer using saw
Puffed face, tree ash, lips shielded
Bracket, arm, vest move steady.

Triumphant woman spinning, arms
Outstretched, fingers reaching like they'll
Pop. Gap teeth big grin sweat on upper lip
Eyes wet and proud. Triumphant woman spinning
Ungraceful and unbridled. In yellow light.

Search.

trope

horizon
noble
figure
leg
canted
aptly
wild
unthreatening
farms
she'll
and
let   her

stabilising
savage
with
aptly
hair
windblown
yet
observe
mutate
explain
go
in

pivot-making
savage
the
kind
struggle
the
kind
cumber
face
seeking
flinch

noble
do
right
of
palm
right
of
her
far-off
yours
away

horizon
leisure
noble
moving
smart
not
harvesting
not
culture
nuclear
bachelor's
stable
good
stare
her

unfeasibly
now
savage
opened
joyous
proud
holden
this
near

lock   her

hurling
legging
savage
glow
but
intellectual
dollars
rich
hushed
family
degree
job
teeth
into
beam

close
noble
teeth
bold
burn
shouldered
provocateur
loud
threat

out
she   is   here

craftwork

this is a heavy-handed poem   Pursue only honesty
about feather-finger   Disguise earnestness
poets who lie to you   Have no agenda but
real good and yeah, so: Artistic furtherance.

sap clot

Tender! Horror!

Thrice 'pon the shore comes the violence;
upon it too, come the corpses, lukewarm by the fern.
Tossed by the sea, fat and soaping
they churn.

Where will you turn, survivor, for guidance?
Kick the slag, mourn the sea,
heave bile at the silence!

Your parts archived in distant places,
mothballed and stern.
Yet, we too are violent women—and violent we learn.

Yes! Tender we strike and shrewdly we yearn.
'Til vengeance or we are wrung out—
our words'll tender the violence
while they
tender violets
in drought.

And us women seeds

both sewn and unseamed by the fray.

footwork

The stride that took our bodies here
Can take you further still

Bind your limbs, sluggish, fearful
Stumble hill come higher ground

Resilience is no buzzword, strength
Will weave you to the suffer rope.
There is no buffer and no toughening
We wear raw we stay alive.

Long, we amble on into and from
Calamities come us to meet.
Since arks, wetlands hawk coughing dust
Sand clings and grows and grows your feet.

But should it ever wash from you
Sans bank or spring or beach
And should madd'ning heat one day
Bring saltwater come brush your reach.

You'll know the stride that took you here
Will bear you well into the breach.

the abattoir

begat bedeath

No more a line of birth than a litany of death brought me into this world.

This is the familiar scene of at least three generations. The sheep's bone is chalk dry and creaks at Dad's touch. With a tug of a cold and numbing hand, the bone's slick enclosure urges it out.

My Pop's on the offal floor, sends the lamb up to my father as a gift— dozens a day like so many traditions would do to acknowledge his entry into the family. This family, all wholesome harvesters of flesh crops. From oesophagus to anus—the body is scoured of any engine that would suggest a lived life, and passed on.

My Nan tends to the hooks that carousel the clean corpses up. They are sanguinated and gutless once she touches them. She presses the euphemistic cavity together like a dull book. Slams the carcass onto its horror transport hook. She is a funereal jester woman, solemnly but portly and with good humour she weaves the dead into their next carbon-cycle phase. With a heave and a bent back, the conveyor shoves them through a plastic curtain.

It's a normal bad day at work. There's a call.

We wait in a car at the gate with devon sandwiches. A truck of cloud-enclosed meat is permitted entry at the door, by my Grandpa—a security guard. One of the cloud lambs breaches the slots of the truck; his face turns to giggle at us, agape. Until I'm home, I can't cry about it.

We were hunters and gatherers and ecological strategists. Our old towns established by gubs to boil down tallow. Now, we gather up backstrap. We hunt cheap supermarket cuts. We adapt, always mediators of the squeamish line between life and the lives we have to take to keep living.

We devon daughters—the first generation who have not killed to live in the new way or the old—sook when we crush an ant. At school, our family's gift is trucked to us on dissection day: a hot heart whose fat is not yet solid.

'Pull at the strings, girls!'

We swear they beat beneath us.

outskirts

Now, the plane lurches.

Tamworth, a blooming outpost, flings up microbursts and wind
from its hills under the eastern, and wealthy, suburbs. Clouds that
seek to pass those hills dump their water to rise past them. The plane
before us diverted from these hills to an airport two hours away; its
passengers followed the rain on its many dripping edges from the hill
to sea level in a top-heavy stale coach.

'Orographic rainfall,' I heard on days like this, watching clouds sluice
up the road in school.

So, the plane lurches through this humid tempest and, unlike it, the
rain is sure and straight and swift. My ride is tossed, indirect yet frank,
through clouds with ten silent passengers. At least it doesn't dump me
to ascend.

We burst through the clouds. I can see the ground. Our shadow
bounces on the abattoir. Its sole leading road is near swamped by the
deluge. It comes up in silver puddles. A truck cuts through them.
Looking up, three workers clung in blue from hair to toenail, are
stretched tall by their reflections. Then, we land. Dumped on the
tarmac, we run to the terminal.

Abattoir Road weaves itself into Wallamore Road. Wallamore Road links
my family's house to town. Wallamore Road dips into Timbumburi
Creek, which gets fatter for the rain and cuts whole suburbs out of the
town. I'm barely dry and barely warm from the tea in my belly, but we
need sausages. Potatoes. Steak. All before Timbumburi does its work.

The car resists our driving and our driving resists the water and the water resists our car. I want to be back on that plane, in the warmth of someone else's fault. When we finally pick up some speed, we're resisted again and swerve and shriek and brake—this time for a woman clad in blue from head to toe.

On a good day, she'd walk. Today, she wades. Her drawn face howls as the car flings Timbumburi Creek onto her. Is she heading home? If so, she has the industrial district to cross before she comes up to anything like a house. I track her walk. Hardware stores, rental car facilities, dog shelters, a CrossFit shed, crematorium. If she's looking for food, she has a residential belt to breach too.

It is a long walk. Long enough for only where there is no alternative. Abattoir workers make roughly seven hundred a week. No bus goes out to the abattoir. Its taboo and scale puts it out of reach of any town infrastructure, and out of moral notice. Seven hundred is not enough to make for a car. So, she walks, and today she wades.

I think of another near-mythical abattoir worker almost by compulsion. That mythical abattoir woman's tale was passed through us as easily as a plate around the table. Always as a plate around a table.

Here's what it brought.

Katherine lived in a nearby town called Aberdeen. She worked the offal floor, slicing up the waste tissue scooped from a carcass to sell for dogs and miscellaneous deviants from the flesh-eating tradition. A job she relished and at which she excelled. Katherine was promoted to boning, where she harvested muscle tissue, gristle and fat from the corpse to be sold at a premium or sold as stew fodder for humans.

At this point of the story, the storyteller scans the table in pause. My father worked the same job. But, a love for the kill is a shadow—especially for a woman. Especially for someone speculated to be an Aboriginal woman. Especially for a possibly-Aboriginal woman who wove the familiar passing tale in late-1960s rural New South Wales, and who wove it to her children.

Anyway, Katherine turned that violence to her husbands, lovers, dogs. Eventually, she killed her husband, skinned him, set the table with her children's placecards. He was served.

We chewed over the story with a steak, quietened by our sudden knowledge of its making. *Kill the cow. Skin him.* We looked at our mums and nans and aunts and other killer women. We knew the lives they had to take to keep us living—an eerie, industrial extension of the lives that kept us living before.

To me now, Katherine's story is so distant it has lost its chill. I reminisce fondly on the town's fascination with it in my youth, its sparse retelling. Our tin car sweeps this woman, like all in the abattoir, so unlike Katherine and yet so worn by her, from her long tread from abattoir to home.

We buy what she made on the other side of town. We have no seat for her.

killwork

Dad scrubs at his shirt and its pink, fatty imprints. They stay. Killwork is an unpleasant task with an unpleasant premise, but its output is widely enjoyed.

Bar a national boycott of animal products, the abattoir will stay a bulwark of rural towns. *The mines, the fields, the meat!* Even as it sits askew and dutifully turned away from polite society, it's hardly invisible.

Abattoirs gurgle their way into public debate. Halal meats are made in specialty abattoirs whose service is regulating kills, and adhering to a common sacred obligation to life. White conspiracy theorists accuse those halal slaughterhouses of lacking transparency or funding violence between humans. I guess they've never seen *this* mean, mainstream, and opaque rural abattoir, perched on a crest far from its fence, for whose task only a trickle of short-term, broken-backed workers can testify. One Nation voters eating its lamb on Australia Day never seen my grandfather's silhouette at sunrise; a security guard quietly coaxing its gates open and shut like a secret heart valve.

In their implied presence, animal rights activists stand there with my grandfather at dawn, pumping the abattoir's blood in other ways to reveal its workings to consumers. Clandestine videos about the mechanics of the slaughterhouse are so common and hard-fought that they went on to define the abattoir fence through litigation on privacy and trespass laws. In 2012, just as the abattoir installed CCTV in response to public pressure, I'd go on to learn about that fence in law school. *Lenah Game Meats v Australian Broadcasting Corporation.* My grandfather learned it through a sign years before. *No photography past this point.*

One such video ended Australian live exports to Indonesia. *A hammer is posed above a tied cow. A cow scrambles over a ramp, its legs inoperable after time at sea in closed quarters.* Barnaby Joyce—once a little-known Senator, now the member for New England and notorious for his dual-citizenship crisis, extramarital dealings and the Canberra root ban—wept about the end to them exports and its impact on our economy. The workers coming through the gate stayed dry-eyed. Who here had heard of an economy that wasn't just keeping the heater off until the windows iced?

Regulating meat is older than the Australian nation-state. For industrial killing, it's as old as refrigeration. Before meat was at its first boom, there came the line-up of meat workers. They throw their jaws out in a show of fitness and temerity. They line up here to bet that the town will be hungry enough for most of them to work that day. When trucks get cold and towns get squeamish about the kill, abattoirs spiral out of orbit into the fringe of society and townships. Abattoirs get euphemised in satellite industry suburbs. The abattoir worker eventually gets sick leave. They can meagrely sustain a family. They eventually get paid for the gross weight of the kill, guts included—so even those with weak arms (but never weak stomachs) can get a slew of assistive and associate quasi-slaughter jobs. *Security. Corpse runners. Offal harvesters. Cleaners!* All indecent jobs with decent pay.

Enter the professionalisation of the town-sustaining kill.

vote

It was 2006. It was Tamworth. We got a Boost Juice. We got a guard of white town councillors, perspiring and with their lives in sunset, who voted to close the town off to new refugees. The town erupted, and Australian media around it.

Five families from Sudan, waiting for resettlement and to join the twelve refugees already there, seemed to disappear in this new bedlam. They were clouded by the spittle.

In this fray, James Treloar, our mayor, told the metro papers to: 'Ask the people at Cronulla if they want more refugees.'

I found out about the Cronulla riots coming home from a friend's house. When my cousins told me, I thought it was a bad joke. That summer, I slowly chewed my lunches and dinners, watching the TV, *the flags, the crowd, the surge.*

Pacing around aimlessly like kids do, never asking Tamworth if it wanted more refugees, I was still told. Cashier gossip at Coles. Running into friends' parents. Older kids paused and whisper-leaning on their bikes. I imagined Cronulla then, imagined asking:

'Do you want more refugees?' 'Refugees fleeing you?' 'Could they come out to here? We have no beaches. We have a big river.'

'Could ours go out there?' Rivers bleeding to a big beach. Refugees fleeing us.

Shifting new migrants and refugees to rural NSW was then a way to regulate the booming population on coastal metropolitan regions and disincentivise coming here at all. Most of the target regions were safe electorates for their worn-in Independents or the National Party. In a gesture that was hoped to quash the national debate, those refugees especially who had suffered across oceans would now suffer this.

'Come out here! No beaches. A big river. A hill. A plain.' 'Six percent Indigenous!'

'Ten percent born overseas.' 'Which overseas?' 'Some outposts from a white island with no real big rivers. No plains. Maybe a meadow.' *'A hill.'*

Tamworth itself had been split neatly in two for as long as John Peel put down his claim for it. Whitefullas burned their thighs straggling up hills in the east to oversee the town. Their homes had pool sheds, thick vanilla multi-wick candles from Byron Bay; the woods in their furniture had names. Blakfullas, regardless of class, smeared us-selves over the vast villages set up at the foothills. Peals of real estate agents avoided Coledale and Westdale, two such villages, said to be populated by 'Vegemites'.

Intermarriage did not bridge what the hill escarped. Blakness was a code embedded in your bones—it didn't bleed *through* you, it constituted you, so there was no letting it out. Like a haunting, all manner of vague racism weighed on you if your nose was too big, your accent too guttural, your step too off. Your spirit and your body made you, just as they condemned you.

So, when the first of the Sudanese refugees arrived, Tamworth's neat race split spiralled. Two kinds of black now—one very new here and one very old. White and blak children on the bus, some no older than six, pressed their noses to the windows like bloodless marshmallows and gawked. Shifted the bus balance while it spun and chafed around roundabouts. Nonplussed, the three men walked on, with a Chicko Roll each, back to their fibro homes. A walk we all did. A house we all had. It was a boring thing to watch.

A white woman in our Vegemite villages—who thought herself besieged by blakfullas already—was doubly affronted by her new neighbours. She would later tell the Sydney Morning Herald even '[t]he Aborigines are scared of them.'

'Come out here! Be welcome! A hill. A plain. A big river. Unsteady buses. Kids. Chicko Rolls.'

'An abattoir.'

The abattoir asked for only three things—capacity, resilience and an implicit agreement not to sue if either gave out under its punishing workload. It offered hard work for not much money, but money all the same. A formula for drawing minorities under the thumb.

Unseemly allies in the context of interracial intra-black friction, although seemly allies on the grander scale of colonisation, the two groups of black workers filled the ranks. They worked together, lunched together, and lived in these same neighbourhoods far from the foot of the hills. In 2005, at the time of the vote, such a job would net a humble pay packet, but its stigma cost would be greater. Treloar and his supporters accused the Sudanese abattoir workers of criminality, violence and disease. We gathered around *A Current Affair* during the fallout of his fateful vote. He said:

'They say to the women workers—hey, you, you're coming home with me!'

The charges were familiar.

Still the children gawked and still the bags were clutched, and I don't know when, but once the novelty ran out, I guess this became an equal-opportunity game on the bodies of blaks and blacks alike. Once the Australia First Party in Tamworth figured out that Aborigines weren't their rooting claim, even after the vote denying the refugee families was rescinded, the white fury escalated and diversified.

Accusations of petty theft, abuse, predation, intimidation. Police attention. Charges of driving without licences. Other perils of a low wage and residence at the foothills. I'm told Tamworth is better, now. I'm told that there are more refugees there and things are okay enough.

I see the abattoir. I see the 2006 newspapers and their vague unfounded threat—men proud at work in fridges with carcasses, in sterile blue gloves from head to sole.

tinker tailor

After carting corpses for most of her adult life, my Nan, a short woman by any measure and with thick, yellowing glasses, was agonised. Her back had worn thin from it, and her face had grown sallow. Once vibrant in all our home videos, she was pale and drained and barely filled her skin.

We drove hundreds of kilometres for her treatment. Went to a place where the traffic split inconceivably (*motorway bridge exit*), where the roads had numbers and costs, almost so loud (*so regular, so constant*) that you could block it out and feel a real silence unlike anything.

Mum explained this to us carefully. In the surgery, Nan lay face down, like one would on a massage table. Instead of kneading through her soft ridged skin, a surgeon undid her seams and knit her some new back stuff.

In the weeks she recovered, our whole extended family let out an apartment in Western Sydney—my first visit to a city at eight years old. When it was time to go, we spiralled our way out using an old map and visits to phone booths to call someone with a better map. Kept ending up in Blacktown.

We paused and stretched our legs behind one particularly long and infuriated and loud public appeal for directions. I saw a reaming street of butchers with red fresh cuts lovingly curated on AstroTurf. I saw a faded poster in a glass council cabinet. Everything had sun-bled out of it, except wordart reading 'Darug'.

Mum read it and said, 'They call this place Blacktown because it was given to two Aboriginal men.' Seemed weird to me that the whole continent wasn't Blacktown.

When we got back in the car, Mum turned to me and said, 'Actually, I heard it was called Blacktown because they gave it to the first Aboriginal doctor, a woman!'

Later, when the local government pushed to change its name to attract the aspirational class, I read that Blacktown was where mob congregated against the apocalypse of early colonisation. A bustling refuge of blak doctors and leaders and preservers. A diaspora headed by the Darug nation, over which our disoriented Toyota kept spiralling.

It took fourteen hours to get home.

I next remember Nan, relieved but tender at home, with a palm on my Pop's big chest.

Now, in her late sixties, she turns from the sterile mess of the abattoir and cleans the homes of those who own them. She is lean and strong and smart, her hard and ready back balanced out by the warmest, nicest belly in the world.

It beats beneath you.

heartwork

of the

Trevorrow v State of South Australia (No. 5) [2007] SASC 285

The forty-nine most common three-word phrases in the judgment of Justice Gray, ranked.

Secretary of the—
the secretary of
the plaintiff is

of the CWPRB
(of the Aborigines)

The Aborigines Act
from their parents.

Aborigines Act 1934
children from their
of the plaintiff.

That the APB
(The Maintenance Act
Act 1934 1939)
the Aborigines Department—

Aboriginal children from
of exemplary damages;
of Aboriginal children;
of the maintenance.

Power to remove.

Maintenance Act 1926.
Of the state,
the Crown Solicitor.

Remove Aboriginal children
to remove Aboriginal,
an Aboriginal child

The minister of
the plaintiff was,
and the CWPRB.

Award of exemplary
of the child
Minister of works
that the plaintiff
Chairman of the
at the child.

Neglected Aboriginal children,
the legal guardian:
Officers of the;
the chairman of;
control of the;
the removal of;
the power to;
legal guardian of.

To the minister,
his natural family.

Section 38 of
The children's,
the plaintiff and—

Conduct of the
Act 1926 1937.

casework

two-barrel parent-tender
sniffle gun, yellow rim

white mum commercial break
relatable, irritable sniffer wipe.
bab kick out and reach.
tissue bumble golden lab
whisper aloe vera. vera

'allo.

two-barrel parent-tender
welfare order. a law-bound
guest at door
a wincing grin.

toys stack into drawers
kettle boils quick
kick sweep the floors
enter clipboard checklist workers

and a coincident great huffing sneeze
from that two-barrel infant yellow gun.

blak mum commercial break
relatable, punishable sniffer wipe.
bab kick out and reach.

ma'am, and your garden's overgrown.

with aloe vera. aloe vera, soothe this
   wrench-ed, watch-ed home.

the errand

In this poem, we kill some ants in a bad way.

Muddied deep in risky bliss that drought has hit
and sprinklers missed.

We're warming, beading, sweetly leading.
petrol hot on the wind casts
haze-shadows, to a keening crowd.

So down a dirt throat that ancient petrol stuff goes, and
although with that, the errand of brutality is
probably
technically
already
done; the spectacle is not.

Local Father strikes and
strikes and strikes and
lights the match; an' like opening a window to catch the sun
summons luminous hell passageway into the earth.

Cosy by a burnoff gas-mining flame,
slow slow burn and vacuum lack
of screams for all this death.

When this ritual's
explained,
bubblin' in his guts like they're the vapour hell below,
Local Toddler lurches and other hells burst free.

Brows singed, blistered hands; a prematurely
roasted lamb.
He bursts, he boils, he screams for the ants.

for feral girls

This one's for the feral girls!
She got that—well, it's cliché—

leopard print, she got that
thigh crumbling rumbling cheek. She got that
river map undie seam.

Nothin' nobler than to end up like the feral girls I knew.

Solemn dread of bush-piggedness hemmed we in—
would we burst, big, ostentatiously?

Like our bellies, butts and cunts
model dimples, stretch marks, noisily.

You got that
chain-smoking habit, Nintendo 64 and KFC for dinner. You got that
hanging out down the main street, every five year off to Port
   Macquarie. You spoke
my language better than me, taller than me. You got high.

Yuself make messy determinations of
care, space, suffering,
joy, sex, sweat, body,
spirit, welfare,
violence, anti-violence, community, culture,
decolonisation, tidda supremacy.

Bush pigs, tight and ugly with panty lines, genital bulges and wiggly
    bits, loud in a Maccas carpark—refusing to bear it all.

'O, youse feral girls,'
Twisting hands, dancing to *warrambul* like they're crossing fingers,
twisting Kmart bras under Big Dub singlets.
They got that
sacred patchwork of precedence—legging thighs follow panty lines,
    topograph their overcourse—goad softly little babs to sleep
goad firecourse to wake
goad Centrelink, its cards and monies, from the settler state.

She shrugs the work of goodness and forgiveness
dare someone pulls her pigtails, she ply the playground 'part with
    vengeance.

Got wind itself as hair. The feral, reviled by whites and upright
    blakfulla alike
got more to tell us—

I'm yet to learn anything your feral girlhood
didn't already know,
nor fight any fight
your feral girlhood wasn't already set to win.

housemade

I'm   jealous.   Leaning   in.
Land   Landing   feet.
Easements,   grant.   scaffolds.   Clean   hands.
Affirming   nods.   What stirs?

She's   free,   me.
Roots   me.   of   Worms   away.
My flat
feet stay.

bathe

Squared against the swoop of sea
four gaayili swoop back them backs.

They grip on work, drive shoulders to arm
power down—sore legs, sore many parts.

Two of the crew shriek saltily
caught, slapped by chain from neck to wrist.

Tears, two salt-wet masses meet.
They meet. Their marinader's hands meat.

Some foaming hell—slime slipping in
suddenly shaken of barnacles.

One body jolts loose.
Churns into the brine.

Three gaayili now cling to the chain
Sing out and *gindama-y, gindama-y*—

'Jayden, first in the drink!'

Maroubra Baths calms, a scrappy head among the churn.

Who's lost his pants, but
hand still gripped on the chain rock fence.

His sibs chortle, dive, dunk him in again.
A weary adult yelps

'Awright cheeky buggers, it's time to go home!'

This is a poem about not suffering.

The History of Sexuality Volume III

I wanna think about desire.
Ground knows I've lamented it;
wax lyricised, wane hypothesised it.

How can two blak women love each other?
Get outside'o that white projection
with Panopticon protecting it all?
Is my want for you pure? Is your want for me?
It's got me worried, sick
to my turgid fingertips.

I mean, I've lyricised hypothesised it yes
little blood little think,
I reckon
I got some reciprocal decolonial desire for you.
But decolonisation is a—
                              —bad metaphor, I know.

                    It's hard with/your mouth on mine/get these
                    sentences/out proper/this whole time; mind
                    whirring deep/listen/no hint we'd/planned
                    this mean thing.

Didn't know what was happening—a totally
unremarkable conversation for us. Deaths in custody?
Sovereignty? Our language, born in us anew?

Is my mouth now bleeding or is
blood just too close to the skin? I don't think
my lips have ever been darker. Oh, wait, were we talking about
whether our law is feminist mobocracy? I didn't know your thoughts
    on that—

—I wanna think about desire. Get that
rash—rations—rational. You said
        fuck.

Huh, I feel you. By the time I

knew what was happening, we were five minutes in.
You bring your jaw up for spit-heavy air.
I hiss *Wiwurra*—like it means a million.

        Wait—what?
        I say *fuck*.

You hesitate.
I wanna.

        Think about that desire. Or, old myths that
        we can't count past five. If we couldn't, how
        could I count the quick quick seconds my
        body plunged into long long biruu when you
        stopped hesitating?

Wiwurra.

Buurralaa garay, lub.

Now I know my mouth is bleeding.
I wanna think about desire.
I wanna know how this moment started
five minutes ago.

Five minutes ago—your finger hairs combed
my procheilon; dumb accident. I think. Someone said
Yeah aw'right shut up.

badwork

shoulder blades to kiss

Build it up.
If it's right way
you can leave
it be set.

Wash yourself.
Scrub your belly
'til it balds
'til it tickles.

Crack your back.
Pull your shoulder
blades to kiss
puff your chest.

Gulp it now.
This is food and
who can say
you'll eat next?

exhibit tab

Inquest into the death of Ms Dhu (11020-14) [2016]

The forty-nine most common three-word phrases in the Western Australia Coroner's findings on the death of Ms Dhu, ranked.

First Class Constable
██████ ████ Dhu
The death of
Of ████ ████
Into the death
Death of ████
Dhu 11020 14

Inquest into the
11020 14 page
████ Dhu 11020
Class Constable Matier

4 August 2014
Senior Constable Burgess
Exhibit 1 tab
3 August 2014
At the inquest
2 August 2014
Exhibit 3 tab

The emergency department
That she was
Am satisfied that
I am satisfied

Lock up keeper
To the effect
The police officers
Exhibit 4 tab

The effect that
's evidence was
Fitness to hold
Evidence was that
Of the police

The fact that
To hold form
Would have been
That she had
The Western Australia

There was no
Emergency department notes

Exhibit 2 tab
The custody system
██████ Dhu's temperature
The police vehicle
Lock up procedure

Ought to have
Western Australia police
Class Constable George
Through his counsel

Was feigning her
Lock up procedures.

sparse shit poem

Heard you
hurtin'—
            got you
            this

                        sparse
                        shit
                        poem.

                                    Helpless
                                    mewling
                                    at the sting.

                                    Offered you
                        as a salve.
                                    Offered us
                                    as bad salvation.

Offered back
as stand-in
turbine. Heartbeat
'lectrons for y'nation.

clockwork

A pencil a lolly stick a whistle.
To arms!
Battle call paddock peers.

The barricades are lush trees and
other lushes.
Errant kids in tight'ning nets.
Their bully mans and mimes the bulliman.

To arms!
Time monsters tweenagers and slips!
Curtain twitchers see scallywags. See
golliwogs, mime blak bogeykids.

and their phones
and their nets
and their bullimen
manned.

app

Her silver brick heralds
chewy news. Urgent orders.
Tea had. Burdens

shared. The app come
bearing its work. Disrupt
Aunty, cousin all

lined up. Them digital plains
buzz and shudder.
Uber, for the everywhen.

Independent contractor
augmented community.
No minimum wage.

No callout fee, a
dockland line up of confid—
—ants. Poet. Doctor. Nurse.

Guard. Professor
Psych. Lawyer.

Tea had. Burden shared.
Mercenaries in wait
for the surge fare.

gatherher

Chubby hands gone taught this dance—
up to fruit, down to coolamon.

Up to nan's fruit bowl change
down to corner store.

And her new dance, pinch and scatter
five-cent seeds.

by another name

1.

sugar. a dark and heavy breast
cream bub puckered and waiting.
milk enough to flood the plain—
or, milk enough to flood
the plain with them.

2.

if you scatter my flour like ash
drag me—screaming—to the river
beneath your willows we can lash
a scone until it red with berry.

3.

after it all, I'm free to go

if I can harden my dress to the hiding
if it won't tear when I crawl back
if I can home them flooded outskirts
sans them pounds—body, ration, cash.

hospo

oi there, lard arsed butter heifer with ya
momentum interdependent tum, huge crooked nose deep philtrum
tiny eyes, slack jaw, three chins. oi there
boong-y slut—bra line legging line spaghetti strap
oi there! hard work getting up hills, huh?
like old Ford Fairmont, heaving townward 'gain today

oi there, feral Cheryl. head toe chicken offal.
oi there, fat slag. need of a service?
or can I buy these chicken carcasses sometime
before I die? six bucks an hour too
much for you, hey   *chortles to the mates*
buck a kilo? this? to feed to my dog?
hey   *chortles to the mates*
hey   *chortles to the mates*

cottonononon

linking yellow electric light cluster to smaller yellow evening cluster
we're hurtling long highway insulated by cushion cotton bulbs.
but there is no harder place. want to open this door, sweep
this. open palm, fingers splayed. comb out them bulbs what fall off
trucks, leavin' the cotton gin. harvest puff nuggets; thistledown.
this harvest is forbidden to me; skim the cream what come from blood.
small family little further on, plucking them to green shopper bags. the
partakers in our small car caravan grimace. two hours other way is Moree is a
cotton gin. minimum wage minus costs every uncle aunt cousin do that seasonal
exploit. gin cotton, gin! wear polyester! with that, on our mind we're hurtling
how long? a highway cushioned by cotton bulbs. there is no harder place.

WORKWEAR

Work wears sometimes in the hands.

Chalk is cheap, but not always cheap enough.
Twist youse—
    grip
     slip
       ya callouses into
pockets, over satin blouse.

Work wears sometimes in the eyes.

Youse sclera is dry and rouging rough,
each eyelash barely reach—
    the dirt
     will sting
ya vacant bulb in cracking drought.

Work wears mostly in the jowls.

Beneath them ya teeth are ground,
yet out of touch—
    a gulping paste
     cement truck belly.
Ya cheeks blotched and slack.

Work wears upon youse.

the pallor the bruise the wound
        going pale,
                press your
blood out.

legwork

stride wide and singed and chafed and out
take on the ache and take it off.

at Daguragu, hundreds clot the creek.
stem the flowing of themselves. horses cramp. abandoned rooms.

wet season, flows go on and off. petitions, courts, and title and such.
from Gurindji and to Gurindji, a fist pours out its dust

no more this back ajar and ready
no more the outpost bloom so steady.

branchstack

no man is an island
blak women in the public service are.

yellowed harbour in a hostile sea
a sharp and wetless fern.

those cast shadeless on their shores
pant and burn.

weaving currents, office floors
island, ward both churn.

busywork

Many hands light work
jobs bring
dignity to mob.

                                Even if forced.

If
they
have ever
I
have never
seen it.
If they pay
some will never know.

I seen plenty work to do
among it so few
dollars.

Who will pay
what needs do, while we must do
what's only sometimes paid?

Them rolling
routines, won't alone sustain
us.

Won't prove our human
ity to shock jocks.

line up

wait	stare	mute
spin	swallow	lighten up
pick	favour	choose
take	arm	savour
hang tight	ache	eat
breathe	piss	weep
pity	harden up	heave
leave &	want &	lose.

the school

not a lake

Lake Keepit rose and fell with El Niño and La Niña like a lung.

When its belly rose, kids joyfully splashed in it. The sky filled with
limbs half-committed to their bodies. Girls were jettisoned from
speedboat-drawn inflatable donuts, got greenstick breaks.

When its belly fell, kids ruefully dipped themselves in it. As El Niño
swept in, we remembered that Lake Keepit was not a lake at all, but a
dam. It strangled our big rivers. Tiny figures tinkered on its towers, my
second third cousins, twice or more removed. Algae, never mentioned
what kind, would clot around you and inhibit free movement. Having
rarely seen a beach, this is what most people in Tamworth thought to
be seaweed. I came to loathe the place during a decade-long drought. I
stood no more than toe-depth, grimacing whenever I was splashed.

I emerge in this dank scene, an earnest pre-teen spiritualist—for that
summer. School breaks. A few of us, subjects of a Baptist Church
outreach youth group, heaved ourselves down to bible camp while
Lake Keepit breathed out. So deep and sated was this particular exhale,
it revealed a sunken memorial to a drowned toddler—now a swamp
figure that would plague our horizon along with the cousin-ants.

Five days, true American-camp style. Log cabin, old hotel art. Hard
race edges and colonial names ran through the buildings and our little
group of twelve pov early high-schoolers. The blak girls organised
ourselves into a cabin named 'Oxley' after a man who traced our
rivers—some now dammed by Keepit itself—to found quaint and
cruel towns on them.

I remember so little of that camp, but for two events.

On the fourth day, a kayak overturned and trapped two girls beneath it for twenty seconds. Our camp pastor, a portly, hand-cream lathering woman, ran to the water and helplessly shrieked until their heads burst through green lake film.

As we all dried by a fire, she said, 'I watched to see your little heads pop up! I was watching, I was. So, so worried, you would die before you were saved.'

The two would-be drowners, one a First-Fleeter descendant and born-again Christian, one an Aboriginal atheist in search of a lake trip, linked eyes. The Christian grimaced.

The last day, my family and the other girls' families came to a barbecue.

I felt proud and holy to be amongst these waters, dammed by the labour of cousin-ants and woven into my story by some brute frontier force. After I ate, I meandered to its shore where the atheist skipped rocks. The cousin-ants skimmed on the dam wall overhead.

She nodded at me in acknowledgement of our mutual feeling. *About this dam*, I thought? *About Oxley? About religion?* All this, in my churning hot pre-teen head, made me do something profound, so I thought.

The cousin-ants told me there was ochre round there. I dipped my hand near the algae-shore and smeared my face like I saw in books.

'What are you doing?' the atheist hissed. 'That's rank!'

'It's—uh, it's ochr—'

The camp pastor hollered and beckoned us back to camp. My unwilling blak accomplice cast an urgent look over her shoulder and pulled me to the water. 'You fucking idiot,' she hissed. 'You fucking idiot!'

Cupped her hands. Gestured for me to do the same. The atheist bucketed my fringe and face with algae water. I caught it with my palms from spilling down my pants. She grunted to me about what ochre really was. It wasn't what she was sluicing off me.

That was pelican shit.

While the pastor trudged down to us, the atheist said, 'I'm not atheist. Everyone's saying I am, but—'

'Well, what are you?' I mumbled through curled-in mouth.

'Hey,' she rapped my forehead. 'You know, you'd know if you'd jus' bloody listen.'

I could see her through my fringe as she pulled away. She did not pity me for my stupid pride, my lure to easy answers. We were both young, colonially-bounded. I was a dam with an algae infestation and a gate made by cousins. She was a lake with inlets, quietly feeding out.

All the same, I felt shame. So, by shame, I was cleansed.

The camp pastor beamed, slowing her pace to appreciate the scene. Me, kneeling and hands clasped and drenched and trying not to cry. So, I was baptised, in her eyes.

lingo

My youngest sister, Katie, a digital native if ever there was one, first spoke Gamilaraay when she was in primary school. While she radiated with sweat under stage lights and broad-shouldered jackets to speak it, from a round-faced bab to a long-faced teenager, I lazily watched on a chair under a vent.

Now, while she luxuriates in her house under a vent, I'm in the aisle seat of a bus some hundreds of kilometres away with an app to get my pronunciation right. I press an English phrase. This thin box speaks it back to me how me gut knows it and how me blood forgot it.

> *Baluwaabadhaay garay guwaala.*
> (Speak slowly please.)

> *Baluwaabadhaay garay guwaala.*
> (Speak slowly please.)

> *Baluwaabadhaay garay guwaala.*
> (Speak slowly please.)

> *Baluwaabadhaay garay guwaala*, sis.

thunderbolt

Thunderbolt worked as a stockman in north-west New South Wales, then as a bushranger, and then he died and worked as a local, cheap-crime folk hero. Mary Ann worked as a blak woman in mid-1800s Mudgee, then taught him basic literacy and her pet operatic delights, and then she died and was forgotten. As I urge through Uralla on the New England Highway, a triumphant statue of the man rears his horse at me in old bronze. Metres away, he made that last career change when he was shot robbing an inn.

I eat my pie dutifully by Thunderbolt. He shares no word of his accomplice. No idea how she ended. No mention of why she taught young Thunderbolt and why no one else did. In the thirteen years after Mary Ann ended their relationship, he never knew of his Aboriginal son. He became a horse trainer for good money, his dad a bronze-horse rider and his mother, after doing everything else, now doing nothing.

Unlike her son, so many more of Mary Ann's mob would be bound to Thunderbolt's fate—stockmen robbed of word and song. And, unlike Thunderbolt, of coin.

mulberries and devon

We would do this. We'd always do that. English's crude grammar—the habitual aspect—makes a nostalgic monster of old routine.

When I say 'we would go picking mulberries', I mean just that. A string of uniform memories drained of sentiment. I want to tell you as it would be.

The barriers are fathomable, and petty, like most small-scale, small-stake youth class tensions seem. My high school, a local Anglican institution split across gender, dressed us in milkmaid pinafores, called us 'ladies', measured our blue-check hemlines to the mid-calf. We already found it hard to shake the cultural memory they re-made in us: virgin treasures of early-settler Tamworth.

Even as we forced our feet around the spoils of the rural upper class—with their three SUVs, guest rooms, granny flats, and TVs so huge they'd make your skull buzz—we looked like girls torn from *Picnic at Hanging Rock*. Local curtain-twitchers would draft complaints to our principal in their heads, dripping manifestos about how girls 'used to behave'.

They and we had fallen for the same trick. Like that, we wandered in from 1900 Kulin bushland, emerging as scholarship povvos and scholarship Abos in 2007 Tamworth East.

Once more with feeling! Again, that damn, half-ashamed, reflective English feeling.

The mulberries represent three rituals. The first one a notional, cosy rebellion—wandering fifty metres from the school. The second, an impulse harvest. The girls with public schoolteacher parents swept mulberry leaves into their backpacks for class silkworms. The third—sensual. A chance to gag and drain chewy mulberries, pick out their tiny bugs, sweep the bug blood and juice on your hands, darken your lips.

Simple, lush and stupid customs get yellow when you paint on them the flatter-lacquer, the past habitual tense. I want to press out that English from those memories, from those Gomeroi students, like I could get juice from a mulberry through them blue-check dresses if I had the guts to stain them.

I only have one real high school yellow memory that's an event, not a tendency, and it's not even mine. My younger sister, Kelly, got the story. Here it is, plain.

Two Aboriginal students, Patricia and Kelly, sit in a playground with a gaggle of other girls. Kelly asks her, 'Ay Trish, what you got for lunch?'

They each pull out devon and tomato sauce sandwiches on white bread.

Patricia grins and says redundantly, but for good emphasis, 'Devon and tomato sauce—ay!' Laughs and laughs and then Kelly laughs.

Whenever we tell this story, its gubba recipients grin-grimace. Do they laugh or don't they?

That's the gag. The joke's about them.

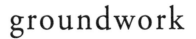

groundwork

the skeleton of the common law

'This Court is not free to adopt rules that accord with contemporary notions of justice and human rights if their adoption would fracture the skeleton of principle which gives the body of our law its shape and internal consistency.'

Mabo v Queensland (No 2) (1992) 175 CLR 1

The forty-nine most common three-word phrases in the Mabo decision, ranked.

The Murray Island—
The Murray Islands.

The common law
(By the Crown
Of the Crown).

New South Wales,
The Meriam people
(Of the Colony
Of the Murray)

Rights and interests
Law—native title

Common law native

Of New South
(In the Crown)

The Privy Council
(Of the Island)

The Land Act
(Of the Meriam)

Governor in council
(The Governor in
The Aboriginal inhabitants)

The colony of
The Crown in
that. The Crown
Act of State.

Lands of the
Inhabitants of the—
—to the Crown.

Interests in land
(Of the Aboriginal
Of the Islands)
Consistent with the—
—the Common wealth
Title of the—
—the Crown to
The rights of—

V Attorney General
For the purpose
Of native title.

Vested in the
The indigenous inhabitants
The native inhabitants

In relation to—
With respect to—
The Crown, the—

Of the native
Racial Discrimination Act
By the common—
The Racial Discrimination

rework

Pull over here, watch some spinning nightly fights reach
across a highway's ribs. At the Kamiloroi Highway's spine
two signs rise and speak and re-speak. Their slur contents impeach
a mountain feature to the west. Move your breath with its outline

at which some racing things have come to rest. Others trudge upon.
Ev'ry night, the sign decries 'Gin's Leap'; and it's replied with scrawl.
On this site, dry cliff, all quiet: the blak re-namers brawlin' on.
White ones sparring back. Write, revise revise revise the sprawl.

Winangala! Your feet depress land story-holdin'.
The sign-ribs come down, back up. It matters, the tale—
whose many versions woven?—woman flees marriage, woman's child stolen.
Your engine paused. Its useless gasps all join the hale

with yours and theirs. See dawn emerge. Your windshield but filmed dust
Gin's Leap de-signed, re-named again. As it must and as you must.

patty

____cake

Three hours. This whimpering car'll get
us to them; Ay there's
steaming beading grasslands. Rise
the lush Pilliga bore baths! Rise!
Through the crispy earth we sog and blush in them.

Is that whole pearly flake immersion
dead skin? Silica worms? Them bore baths cook, water pour in.
    A steady kettle mouth—
Gary selling pool noodles by his trailer.
Them and you unfold real quick; cheap, dissolving as we steep.

A donut bore bath. Expanse so vast the hills don't
block out. Yellow, and all the kinds of blue and green that gubs
    can't see.
Lucky me. On this vast encoding light, decoding grass sweeps.
    A clotted pastry brush.
I'm wet, I'm egg and butter.

beef_____

Five hours. This huffin' car got us to and past the bore baths.
    Lover, look!
A hawk hard arch hover by a railway line—say
'Cute! What is it doing?'

Seeing harder things, adjacent highway. One possum not-so-
    clean in half,
its bub two metres roadward—flat and desiccate.

Eating chicken sandwiches. Dry, don't talk about it.

We kill things to live; respect their body, spirit give us.
I am squeamish. I have weak hands.
Sustain me by proxy kills,
fumble fingers in supermarket shelves.
What spirit going; where lands?

I ate Coles roo. I thought it ethical—
but I found out even they're farmed animals,
reined in on these plains.

Now I glumly eat it all. Cook it up for my gub lover
tight brown steaks naked in bed.
Hold this small hope—my aunt once said
'If you ever wanna know someone's character,
watch how they treat flies!'

I am squeamish and I have weak hands.
My lover cups the buzzing brute
guides it out the window.

_____melon

Pademelon.
A small marsupial.

Paddymelon.
A round, hard fruit to throw at mates.

Which means black bruises on your chest
and also deep and coursing skies
arranging your blood for all to see.
And bilirubin. Which also means me.

Which also means the bursting stack
of paddymelons thrown at your back,
of playfights, playsex, and all like plays.

Of violence rushing to the river. The river going on. *Warrambul.*

Which also means the overcourse
which also means the Milky Way.
which also means a lit-up night. Go home
when town hills hit back bright.
Finding their loud and empty light
wherever your bags set down.

Which also means a thirsty houseplant
brittle fingers catching sun.

And something like living on despite,
which also means not killing flies.
Treating them good, hiding them food.

Which also means us. Which also means—
thirsty, fingers deep, coursing in your thighs.

Which also means
bruises,
means
paddymelons.

palimpsest

A body was snatched by a bigger moon. Superimposed, this plaque. From *Gunnerah* From *shaken deathbed confession* to *book highway*. The plaque got this word on where he sits. In an archive We lap at the ground. Our language while I learn it. Something languid winds

It sitting upright. It tree lovingly gouged. to *Red Kangaroo* from *Red Kangaroo* to *Red Chief*. to *tourist information centre attraction* off a softer relief portrait in profile. It sits him up. I've now no drawer, wrapped in his tongue and then with theirs. mutters out of a linguist. I wait for a translation out of it.

The plaque reads—

Yilambu giwihr gayir Kambu Gunirah gir ginyi. Ngihrngu mari ngihrma gayir gaweh Canuhr. Ngihrma binal wuraya, wahrunggul yiliyan maringu Gunidahngu ginyi.

In times past there was an Aboriginal man called Cumbo Gunnerah His people called him The Red Kangaroo. He was a clever chief and a mighty fighter (this man from Gunnedah)

Yirahla ganu wunda dawandah nahbu gayir gaweh Gawinbara Wuraya.

Later, the white people of this place called him The Red Chief.

yardwork

many-breasted field now
phlegmless lawn—

shorn your ways
to the bone.

mow further on.

selfwork

ethnomathematics

one   one

                       none

        half

                               halfhalfhalf

                                              threequarters

                                                              onequarter

                       threequarters

                                                      half

                                              fiveeighths

intact
intractable

teamwork

ONLY	THE	SIB	WE
BLAK	REST,	AND	COMMUNE
MEN	BACK	SIS	IN
	BONES.		
ARE	MINERAL	(WITH	SECRET.
COMMU	SEAMS	EXACTLY	BACKS
NITY.			
	DEPOSI	THOSE	NAKED.
	TED		
	TO	NAMES)	EACH
	BEND,	ARE	VERTEB
			RAE
	TO	SPOKEN	CRACK
			ED.
	SHIELD	LIKE	
	THEIR	THIS:	NURTURE
	MOTION	COMMUN	THE
		ITY'S RE	
		SOURCE	
	AND	COMMUN	THREAT.
		ITY'S POTENT	
		IAL.	
	THEIR		OUR
		ORE.	
	MESSAGES.		DRESSAGE
			JUST
			PRESAGES.

greenstick two

With grim hands, find
the clasp, and unhook
unwieldy mirror
unwieldy eyes, unwieldy
forms.

Is this an unmoored body?
Hardly. There's unmoored
cruelty charting through this mud.
Seizing tongues, hopes and flesh
training soft and sapling selves to wilt.

It plants a hedge maze. Its shadow
cast at day's end, grey. It plants a birch in green.

What violent notions growing with that tree?
What gender leaving in its wake for you?

Maybe only the yarraan know
how orange, blue and mauve refract.

Maybe only the yarraan know
what saplings grow to push it back.

Plant a plain, thick garden,
let it choke your lawn
in it, let it live; a possibility; a breath.

Long away, a lonely lung
sucks it in a hasting breast.

Find them. By torchlight we
plant ourselves. Heels and
sneakers. Old earth
grows.
Now, then, and e—

       —ternally, siblings.

the call

post dawn eight seventeen landline
chimes are shotgun pellets hello im just
headin out with the fuck are you hold on i
know on my way i love you too bye wha
oh okay bye no what huh no no i think i
think no his hair always looked like that

bloodwork

Me as blood.

To get to the fruit you go to the root. A sum of grandparents,
    great-grandparents—
a sum of great-great-great-grandparents *great barrel great throat great*
    parent. To quandong seeds, chewed and strewn.
By chaos. Its resourcefulness. A trembling loner among corpses.
And me, her cold and milky tea. A leaf-strewn mudflat under horses.
A tea bag haemorrhaging 'round its spoon. Its leaves flee, remorselessly.

Me as community.

As laterality. A scrambling haze of screaming ants come waft to me
on the wind. A furtive little note, for a knowing nose. Gather tea and
we'll disclose. Or a feud or a veto.

Meet and declare at our splitting root where quandong dragged by
gleeful ants who sing their smell then sign. And certify. To confirm. To
affirm me.

Me as integral self.

A certainty. An insecurity. Some downturned authenticity. Come to
confront the self.

And me, her cold and milky tea and all that it connotes. A wait for the
pathology. To think myself—so small alone—is all my blood denotes.

at Lowes!

We're giving them away!

Fifteen-year-old Murris with short sides and bronze beach tips.
Got their slug-slick polyester ties—*eight dollars!*—and beaming, his
lilac suit shirt! Shock your mates with these smart shoes, black sock
combo—*thirty dollars!* Men's suits—*just ninety!*

At Lowes!

All-ages Koori mall rats cluck at and finger the racks. Thick flannels
only half-printed. They'll do, buttoned-up. Opened, they'll gape and
gasp your race and class.

At Lowes!

Always with a down and plastic sheen. Bubs gleaming in backyard
clothesline formal shoots. Adults make-up jawed and glazed at
weddings.

At Lowes!

Catching sunsets and bouncing them back.

At Lowes!

skin (v)

Skin the mudhay by taking it off
wear its given skin, acknowledging this:
a flesh cog of something bigger.

Skin the human. Strip the possum
and name yulay in its place.

Border.

Talk skin like
something other than
big rubber home
flapping empty organ
referee passport spacesuit.

Red card me
render me stateless
boil me without heat.

Skin me meat me
get courage
really touch me.

goodwork

come spit on me

Dhubi-li come spit on me

Come *gli-gi* this itch in me

Ah so much *ngaru-gi* from me

I've nothing for you but *bawi-li*.

workmanship

heavy weaving hall of men
go in shadow, get bearded-eyed.

shake some hands, handsome shakes, some ministers.
good-natured chuckle, laugh, pat the forearm.

the corridor men chew them smiles.
them family yawp, them decades gnaw.

a popping pipe past the cellar floor. and with his teeth gnashed thin
and short
aghast Unc here's the first in line. to thumb the depths, to be them
plumber.

badblak

there are no instructions yet everything
is formulaic about it being a badblak
grown up you growing up among
gut knowledge among mitochondria
hypochondria the powerhouse of the
cell you were trained in knowing how
easy you are to loathe even the wrap
around of love that grits its teeth and
co-opts principle to survive you does
not shake this

momentum so when you are screeched at on the bus
you are appalled but not surprised when you tread
your way home on a familiar path obscured by
someone's freehold you do not recognise your desire
to walk on when you're awake at eight pm when
the world skips and repeats its gory bits and repeats

its gory bits and you are not perturbed
you go dull this is your place,

Indigene, slip through the world Aboriginally this is your line, as your
    parents will prepare
you so too will you prepare yourself so too you will prepare yourself so
    too will you repair you
are the foundation of whatever's put itself here now—badblak
    worseblak worstblak.

tea & tobacco

A love for two leaves
sticks itself to us.

Bind me to you
bring me
them twin rations. Daughter,

pay me
nothing,
and still I
will
build youse.

Soak me
something,
a leaf. Another
land's. Leave.

Tell me 'bout their
tea-bringing ghost.

We will sip that
soak from another's hand.

Pass me
that lighter.
And still I
will leave
you another's breath
leaf. Breathe you
that ghost's vessel cloud.
Leave my breast,
cross this vast Pacific
sea.

beneviolence

THIS IS *GOOD* FOR YOU!
THIS IS FOR *YOUR* GOOD. YOUR OWN
GOOD. THIS IS FOR *YOU*.

FOR THIS GOOD, IS YOU. IS *YOU* GOOD? GOOD.
IS THIS GOOD? IS GOOD?
YOU IS GOOD FOR *THIS. OWN* THIS!

FOR *YOU*, THIS IS GOOD.
FOR GOOD. FOR *YOU IS* GOOD. FOR
YOUR OWN, YOU OWN THIS GOOD.

THIS GOOD IS FOR YOU.

suffer them sacred children

This balmy interventionist circumstance
scream-marbling. A wince-bubbled broadcast. Gingerly, in come kindly army.

Fought a lawn strategy; mow a plump crop down for chaff.
Burnoff hands and arms, feet and hair, char the raphe.
Guts rendered, soothsayers sizing up the offal graph.

Oversight bodies murmur 'bout the precedent
survivors howl at the fire, askin' where the water went.

comparative

their fervours. dreams
giving you fevers.
their fevers giving
you fewer. their
fervours, learning. moving.

their dreams giving
us fevers. their
fevers giving us
fewer. their fervours,
learning. they dream.
they learn. their—

the centre

futures. excellence.

For people so put out on the fringes, we blaks love the centre. And so, I suppose at some juncture in the late twentieth century, we decided to build our own. Hundreds of them.

The National Centre for Indigenous Excellence is one centre bulb—built up on the suburb of Redfern on Gadigal land, and on the site of a former primary school now turfed to the Indigenous services industry. When I walk under it, my eyes trained on its looming insignia, my jaw tilts to the sky.

I concede that's probably its goal: an Aboriginal woman, proud-jawed, looking to the sky. But it's an earnest and uncomfortable thing to do, and on dulce de leche afternoons it burns my eyes and slows my feet. Pedestrians plunge past me. Sighs knock out of them. My throat is exposed.

As I brush past, a red skybound something winks through to my squint. There it is!

Bounced through a low-hanging satellite that competes with the atmosphere like I compete with the pedestrians, the Centre for Mob Futures is being rebuilt. Far from here, out desert ways, I've reported on its programmers quick to plug its many hostile haemorrhages and rework its paper scaffolds. An archive of drives all buzzing with unsteady fans and unlabelled wires. Lives and lands. Supply missions, of a sort, will soon feed up the data from this sluggish ground cloud and bounce it back around the continent to its makers. While it's out of commission, I can only reflect on its own impact, its own territory.

blak captcha

I remember my first time in the digital coolamon.

Right after the first denial of service (DOS) attack on the Centre, I created a visiting Indigenous account. My work pass would get me in easy and race-neutral, but I felt uneasy entering as an outsider.

The Centre for Mob Futures user registration declined my Confirmation of Aboriginality: at the time, both a refreshing and a disconcerting thing. Instead, it chewed up a perfectly good afternoon with an authentication yarn, something its blak-developed algorithm learned for itself, albeit imperfectly.

'Whose mob?'

Four hours into the nodding and riffing, I made myself a cuppa. Pinched the bridge of my nose. Made vague listening noises. Hot water, splash milk, splash tap water, no sugar, bag in.

Blak Captcha trailed off mid-sentence. 'So, gonna make one for me or what?"

'What, can't get your own?'

'Thanks for affirming.'

'Seriously? Are you serious?'

'Yes.'

I wrote on my hand: *Prob-matic? Tea cliché srsly o'done.* I plugged in. I logged in.

Before I stepped across the Centre's threshold for the first time, the AI put their palm on my belly. 'Sorry sis. You understand, after the DOS. Anyone could be a... y'know.'

'Gub?'

Ruefully, 'Ha. Or a tea-making cliché.'

virtualisation

Mob Futures was 'the Centre to End All Centres!' It was born of some cruel, overlapping coincidences that turned our spears around. The first: mob's big-time mapping and data collecting, beginning with the everywhen and ending with the archive. The second: governments and conservation organisations scrambling over decades to fortify a continent besieged by fire, starvation and water. As the rivers and beaches variously flooded and depleted, cultural competence rinsed in and dried as the high-water mark. Precipitating this policy mineral salt, a clawing to preserve the first Australian for the last one.

What began as an autonomous project, gathered steam and government buy-in as a new kind of protectionist mission; the one we made ourselves. And it was barely a reserve; after all, the Centre recreated the whole continent through cloud computing. It was a parallel world.

But raw data were equipped only to bridge so far. As the population of the Centre grew through government recruitment drives, fostering and resource quarantining, so too grew the Centre's many uncanny yaws and gaps. A colonised continent was one horror. A half-done one that reports to Parliament bi-annually, lived like a reconciliatory fever dream, a waiting room full of pamphlets all at once shouting: 'Be Deadly! Yarn up! You mob!'

I heard enough to be ready when they began to persuade those they couldn't recruit. Who would want to be plugged in to that place, with its eerie flesh goannas? Could I be among a glitch that went and ripped the floodplains dry? I resolved to stay in solid form.

The Centre downloaded my neighbours—voluntarily—not long after the pressure started. They shrugged in resignation on a humid Tuesday morning when the Telstra guy came round. He tinkered with some cords and dishes out on their veranda.

'Witness my signature?' the older woman asked, as she turned from his half-exposed arse.

It was only one piece of paper, single-sided. I turned it over in my hands enough to get its edges sweaty. 'Are you sure? Really sure?'

'I jus' know where it's headed. Booked that idiot two weeks ago. You'd better mind that yuself.' She gripped my hand, forced her pen into it. 'They take a bloody long while to turn up, but they always come eventually.'

The Telstra guy righted himself, hitched his pants, and reached for the contract. I signed it. I said, 'See you later.' I left.

I walked home that night abuzz and sore, the satellite close above me like never before. My ear to our shared wall at dinner, I heard only respirators from next door.

I got a good, niche, skilled government job, moved to a place in an under-policed, unquarantined gub suburb. Still the satellite, bouncing more and more uploads by the day, winked above me every evening. I networked and learned my way around wines and cheeses and small-talk lies about Berlin and Venice. I was getting in to that Centre. I had to see it for myself. I just needed enough critical gub mass to get me out of it again.

I heard murmurs, good and bad. The Centre was a place of contradictions. It brutalised and sustained everything.

Here, totally unsupervised by mission managers—old and new alike— mob frolicked, philosophised, borned art, and built technologies. Reif said the language of therapy triumphed in the West. Ordeal made traumatised subjects, made individual intervention. In the Centre, a place spinning imprecisely through the sky and broadcasting to a supercomputer in the desert, therapy got the language of sovereignty instead. Foucault would also be happy—the Centre's subjects were disciplined and punished to set the terrain for their sovereign joy. Like we'd been trained to do for centuries, the natives could be, and be gone.

Some were there permanently, fostered in for life, sentenced for rabble rousing, fines or debt, or entrapped in the carceral whirlpool, others were on cautions 'for a few weeks', pending a hearing.

In those early days, I was a journalist in an identified position covering the policy era of virtualisation, itself some combination of cultural competency and the last vestiges of the Frontier Wars' benevolence.

Virtualisation stumbled following the DOS. It became difficult to justify the vulnerability of the digital. White nationalists from the meatlands could more or less lay ruin to whole peoples, whole worlds, without so much as a whimper. Continue, though, virtualisation did. So, within a year of the ingratiating wine-talk, I was sent to cover it.

'Your first "on the ground" assignment! Of course, I mean, the cloud.'

I got a temporary pass to the Centre. Social workers, nurses, lawyers, too, passed through these digital gates, all with assurances of non-retention.

I was not the first journalist to come, but I was the first not to stay long.

the last project

I was there enough. It took time. I made friends with Blak Captcha and most of the Centre's residents. And I was on that blinking slipstream surfer to see it collapse.

On that final project, the public broadcaster engaged me to interview the Mob Futures' Council for a documentary series on virtualisation. The series itself was refreshingly autonomous; a rarity in the public sector, thanks to the Centre's hostility to outside reportage. Even if gubs were allowed in, they would have been useless. English petered out towards the end. We, interviewer and interviewees, spoke in Gumbaynggirr, which only a few of us spoke well, but we all knew scrappily.

The last day, I entered and could speak to no one. After a few minutes pacing at our meeting place, Aunty gave me only one comment to pass on, on a written note file, and in English. I remember gawking, her silent, urgent arm grip. I especially remember that Aunty never replied to my goodbye.

I mentioned the note to Blak Captcha. They read it and shrugged. As I slipped back past the belly-touching AI into the real meatland, all sparse and beige-hot and withering, the Centre's satellite lost its signal. It shut down.

There were no alarms. Only one noise signalled our return. I can't place it or forget it. Was Blak Captcha screaming or cheering?

I never got a chance to pass Aunty's comment to the broadcaster before its functions were divided up amongst our nations. Just kept that camera rolling while the rains came and the slow, dull, instinctive work of rebuilding began.

Went back to my old street, overheard the neighbours' yarns and their stupid cliché kettle, and drove on.

I printed the note. It felt significant. It sweated long in my pocket while I waited for somewhere to put it.

I get out of the foot traffic and the sun. I uncurl the note against a wall beneath the arch at the National Centre for Indigenous Excellence. It fit and it sticks, so I guess it stays.

'We're coming back, daught. There's work to do.'

guesswork

Gawn.
    'Close! Don't swallow it
           it's gone.'

Gawn.
    'No, say it like—
    done, like done, ready?'

Gun.
    'Done.'   'Done. Gone.'

Dun.   *Done. Gawn.*
    'Now, say it like done.'   'Done. Gone.'

Gon.   *Done. Gone.*
    'Close, again.   'Dun. Gon.'
    Done.'

Done.   *Done. Gone.*
    'Gone.'   'Now say, Gamilaraay.'

Gon.   *Garmil-arraiy.*
    'Done. Gone.'   'Close! Swallow it.'
Dun. Gon.

                Gamil-arrie.
                  'Like gawn.'

                Gone. Gamilaroi.
                    'Like gawn, dun.'

                Gamilaraay.

                Gawn gone.

gatcctccat atacaacggt atctccacct caggtttaga **don't** tctcaacaac ggaaccattg ccgacatgag acagttaggt **mind**
atgtcgaga gttacaagct aaaacgagca gtagtcagct ctgcatctga agccgctgaa **me,** gttctactaa gggtggataa **I'm**
catcatccgt gcaagaccaa gaaccgccaa tagacaacat **just** atgtaacata tttaggatat acctcgaaaa taataaaccg
ccacactgtc attattataa **here** ttagaaacag aacgcaaaaa **to** ttatccacta tataattcaa agacgcgaaa aaaaagaac **answer**
aacgcgtcat agaactttg **questions** gcaattcgcg tcacaaataa atttggcaa cttatgtttc ctcttcggagc **you** agtactcgag
ccctgtctca agaatgtaat aataccatc **never** gtaggtatgg ttaaagatag catctccaca acctcaaagc tccttgccga
gagtcgccct **asked.** ccttgtcga gtaatttca cttttcatat gagaacttat ttcttattc ttactctca catcctgtag tgattgacac
tgcaacagcc accatcacta gaagaacaga acaattactt **are** aatagaaaaa ttatatcttc **you** ctcgaaacga tttcctgctt
ccaacatcta cgtatatcaa gaagcattca cttaccatga cacagcttca gatttcatta ttgctgacag ctactatatc actactccat **really**
ctagtagtgg ccacgcccta tgaggcatat **an** cctatcggaa aacaataccc **old** cccagtggca agagtcaatg aatcgtttac
atttcaaatt tccaatgata cctataaatc gtctgtagac aagacagctc aaataacata caatgcttc gactacccga gctggctttc
gtttgactct agttctagaa **culture?** cgttctcagg tgaaccttct tctgacttac tatctgatgc **why** gaacaccacg ttgtatttca
atgtaatact cgagggtacg gactctgccg acagcacgtc tttgaacaat **are** acataccaat tgttgttac aaaccgtcca tccatcctgc
tatcgtcaga tttcaatcta **your** ttggcgttgt taaaaaacta tggttatact aacggcaaaa agcctcgaa actagatcct **sinuses**
aatgaagtct tcaacgtgac ttttgaccgt tcaatgttca ctaacgaaga atccattgtg **so** tcgtattacg gacgttctca **big?** gttgtataat
gcgccgttac ccaattggct gttcttcgat tctggcgagt tcggacggca ccgggataa actcgggat tgctccagaa
acaagctaca gtttgtcat catcgctaca gacattgaag ctattcaaaa tagtttgata atcaacgtta **don't** ctgacacagg taacgtttca
tatgacttac acttattgga tgctccagac **mind** tgctccagac tagataatgc taccatttcc gggtctgtcc cagatgaatt actcggtaag

ngaya aactccaatc ctgccaattt **I'm** ttctgtgtcc attatgata cttatggtga tgtgatttat ttcaacttcg aagtgtctc cacaacggat

ttgttgcca ttagttctct tcccaatatt **just** aacgctacaa gggggtgaatg **ngiilay** gttctcctac **with** tatttttgc aagaccatga

walanduur ctgggtgaaa ttccaatcat ctaatttaac attagctgga aagtgccca agaatttcga **questions** caagcttca

ttaggtttga aagcgaacca aggttcacaa tctcaagagc atatttttaa catcattggc **no** atggattcaa agataactca **answers**

ctcaaaccac agtgcgaatg caacgtccac **but** aagaagttct caccactcca cctcaacaag ttcttacaca tcttctactt acactgcaaa

aatttcttct **I** acctccgctg ctgctacttc ttctgtctcca gcagcggtgc cagcagccaa taaaactca **will** tctcacaata aaaaagcagt

agcaattgcg tgcggtgttg ctatcccatt aggcgttatc ctagtagctc **build** tcatttgctt cctaatattc tggagacgca gaagggaaaa

tccagacgat gaaaacttac cgcatgtat **you** tagtggacct gatttgaata atcctgcaaa taaaccaaat **keep** caagaaaacg

ctacacttt gaacaacccc tttgatgatg atgcttcctc gtacgatgat acttcaatag caagaagatt **you** ggctgcttttg aacacttga

aatggataaa ccactctgcc actgaatctg atatttccag cgtggatgaa aagagagatt cctcatcagg tatgaataca tacaatgatc

agttccaatc ccaaagtaaa gaagaattat tagcaaaacc cccagacag **bulayrr.** cctccagaga tgaccacag aataggtctt

tgacccacag aataggtctt

ologist

bury them where the digitabloid blasts
will never find them.

where the pensive
aborig'ne-ologists won't go.

bury them
astride the savage, noble and the vital, and
while you're at it
bury me in there with all them rioters.

discover nothing.

wary them of building all their buildings
grunt at their football fields
groan their pubs and shops to woe.

and bury them with silence when you meet their joyful whooping

withdraw your soil their roots will show.

the mines stay down, you keep the spark
it's okay to find things out.
to stumble, to be wrong, to be resisted, to be slow.

endure it, and forgive.

you are buried where no ologist'll go.
so, we know and you will come to know.

Aboriginal Lands Council

*cal*culated
t*al*c *al*chemy

b*al*conies,
*al*coves

preca*l*culi,
its
m*al*contents

anim*al*culum

shamejob

cocked ankle, warble.
eye flit to me knee
shame perch on shoulder
feel heavy there? it does for me.

turn me eyes out the window.
cuz, it's a comfortable way
for us to talk. get in my car, we'll
swoop around. we shame
and when we shame
the shame job's done:
both sharp and soft like dread.

bowed head, warble
cocked ankle. weapon
hostaging this clenching chest.

shame trace us where we need be led.

framework

light	*emitting art*	fibre	*tug*	grass	*in*
art.	*art*	engineers	*an*	unnatural natural	*state.*
engineering	*is*	an	*art*	of	*the*
natural forces. no more.	*expert*	tids!—	*weave*	dilly	*with*
me.	*a*	committee	*meeting*	with yellow	*landscapes*
to unmeet others,	*to ask—*	how	*do*	we	*arrange*
you	*to*	carry	*you*	with	*us—*
and	*how*	are	*we*	thus	*arranged?*

whichway Asimov

>> **you start here: ground**
>> take code from the rivers, grasses
>> where they divert, so shall you assert.
>>   so shall you be. exponentially.

>> **you will live like: systems**
>> feed die build, feed die build
>> no need for better faster cheaper
>>   no need but what was; what comes next.

>> **you end here: fend!**
>> entropic algorithm, take your back
>> against what: your task to know.

don't @ me

curated tweets

Blak women are
powerful, over-worked and under-praised
Bilingual and trilingual
Oh
I'm getting roots in
Sustain me, sustain me

No suspicious circumstances
Significant overrepresentation
What's native title worth
In a compromised position to sovereignty?
Significant underrepresentation?
No contact with the family?

BREAKING
Individual pathology
Inquest into the death of
2 in every 25

Yesssssss
This hurts
When kids are locked up

Taught through more brutality
Just how disposable they are
Threat to private property

Counternarrative:
Joyous, precious and worthy
I'm not crying—you're crying

I'm not booking flights at my hotdesk
I'm not calling mum at my hotdesk

Love this country or leave it so
Free domestic flights for Indigenous people?
A whole plane full of silent, terrified people in plaid
staring ever forward
Their model of shame on ours

Hmm. My hot take?
The same flat rhetoric

Oh—and wildflowers on the train
Blak women have not been silent
Huge if true.

start-up

Hear me out; we can
synergise them alternate
labour markets.

You know what ones.

Sharing economies
taken from
locked-in populations
innovated upon by
blue-sky nations.

There's no fault in it.

We can
share what is ours—a little
      diversified-economy post-mining boom,
      blak resources *are* primed to renew, a little
      revitalisation of that
      reconciliational foundational work.

There's work to be done. They'd sure be grateful
if we'd leverage their food, get their kids to boarding schools.
      Teach them English and programmin'
      learn lingo—'deadly', 'mob', 'yarn', and 'gammon'.
      Get to them with soft cultural competence, and then
      in fifty years, remember how to say 'sorry'.

Think of what we could build together
if only we just get a little
sway on 'em, a little
clout.

Hear me out.
Like Uber for 1788 synergies.

Why start-up what's already our expertise?

futurefear

Driverless Cars Transmogriphy Ethics!
Galahs spring-grapple from nest to road.

AI Writing Festive Songs!
A puff and it is nothing—some down

Will Automation Take Your Job?
affixed on a rear-view screen. A silent car

Social Media Is Isolating Us!
huffing old carbon.

Piston-punching rolls us on. White frightful
future imaginings. Tailoring the monsters
it needs to fight. That fever whispers half-alive.
Spiral down in clickbait late Monday
afternoon. Read a listicle, futurefear.
Speculative spectacle drawin' near.

S'arvo
I'm watching livestream of kids whose
Great great great great great greats
Saw something worse on their horizon
than automated zombie.

A lineup of kids, tellin' trauma to a
Live inquiry. A flurry of 'likes' an'
'angery reacts only'.
Whole alien nation watchin' obliquely
with no one to hear. They return to
their cells with a future to fear.

scissors anchor pistol

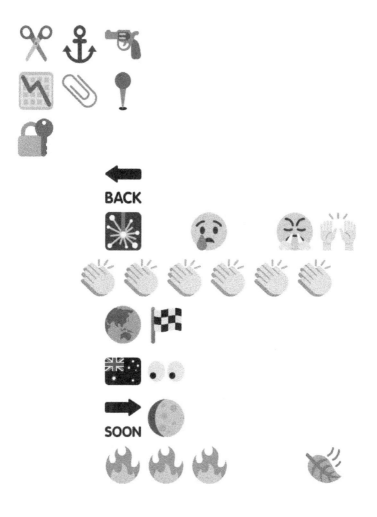

drive thru

I take a drive-thru loop   *near a sulph'rous well*   *a frontier state*
Ten nuggets   *round a zany maelstrom—*   *a hair-foamed bowl*
I'll have an extra sauce.   *radio show. a larrikin's shave and*
No, not that one.   *Waltz Matilda understate, meant a tree to fell.*

Meant a tree is felled.

163

space junk

Orbiting cosmic trash,
    (ejected for momentum's sake,
    broken, fuel-less tools,
    collateral rolling by the wake)
hovers and blocks space townships, neon dreams. A nuisance
catching light and glory briefly. Cheeky, winking back
looms in slow spiral kinship with the deep black.

blakwork

greenstick one

dawnin', darling! eye the dawnin'
although your branches and bones shake
apart with effort, and ankles yawnin'—
them rusty traps—your hinges ache.

though from your toes, you're dipped in dread
from your split ends, in hopeless wonder
and from within, you're lined with sand—

you are inevitable, ahead
of unpredictability; thunder
hard and rolling 'bove the land.

murrispacetime

From me *don't take from me* what this what I been learnin' slowly. Seein' time *stretch out from me* don't take it. I'm seein' slow-stretch-time stretch time before me. *Don't stretch away from me just yet.* Take time.

You're learnin' stretchin' my churnin'. Clear me burn-burly knees just *don't take what I been slow learnin' from me.* Take it from the ██. *From the* ██ *stretch me*—I'm learnin'—

But not from me. An' not from tall buildings—they knit *tie me up at me knees*—an' *not short squat ones made from stones near the sea.* So, shatter them all—*re-knit me knees.* Don't take just them and not just from me. What I'm slowly learning *is that I am not learning* even now even still even soon *I'm stupid.* So, stretch slowly, stupid. *Just don't take it from me.*

Take it from them *them who knew just* what M C an' E can do—before you-know- an' I-think-I-know-who. *I know who the* ██ *is for.* Who stretch it so made. *Who don't take it away.* The ██ stretch *not to cede* just to bounce me back *drag me by me knees.* Don't shatter it please.

build nothing
an' seethe.

See time see I'm learning slow so show. *Stow ya yearnin'* knit together with me. Crack me knees *milk me to the trees.*

The slower I get the less I lead. The more I stupid slowly learn the less I know I need to know. Concede to know to learn. Stretch me elastic *bounce back me and flow.* I am less scared *more ready for scarred knees* more snorted at *more steady*—the more I'm slow *the more I'm slowly stretching back.* Timeless future gone lean on my back.

The further I carry it the less I dream *the more shattered I am by the growing sea* the more knitted I am to the horror tree *the more ready* the more ready *the more made* the more free. Don't take that from me.

I'm from it who from slow knit made me made *slow knit of something just from nothing just.*

survival day

These are the instructions set out for you,
creaseless on your bed this morning:

> make yourself smooth
> fill your caverns
> trap the bugs all in your amber
>
> melt your sandstone
> fuse your backbone
>
> sand down even your crescendos

WHITEWORK

Send in babs with bursting pademelon eyes.
Employ one—casual, entry-level.

Send them aching or,
get them aching and—actually.
Take them—photos of them!—put them
in annual reports.

Send out them acknowledgements,
keep them in our thoughts—I know!

Get them land work,
yeah, get them their land to work!

Spiritual connection can
reach over fences—can, it can
get us to where they can't go.

Ay sis,
they got that capital flow—mapped deep in their rivers.
Let's see how much we can get them to give us.

We got that—gestural forgiveness, we got that
picket line to the heart to get us a wage. We got them
soft currencies, guilt and reconciliation. We got that
land rights panic hustle; unstable fears of the flash.

We got that—fresh mission manager
new ways to indenture
emotional, cultural interns.

They'll get simply no stake in your freehold, Peter.
But, we can probably get that RAP to.

So, there's committees, new buildings, and studies to
make!

Autonomously, they'll do it for low pay—no pay
'til another new thing needs another new name.

Get whitework paid out in cash.

steelworks

the final hour creeps in cold
my panting husk car drags its way
in vague 's' shapes
as if hissing, round dappled hill
and northwest plains on fire

the final hour grips its hold
it's getting pink and orange, grey
makes leadlights of bug guts
lit and lemon on the grill
there's a half-crushed, crepe-winged flyer—
wind-revived—headed home, too

the final hour seems to fold
like dappled liq'rice, on itself
on slopes, my car is briefly stalled with effort
near country, electric, hand frosted by a fan
a pelvic anticipation loiters

now

I've tripped the border wire

                                   car belly on fire.

in ya gut

The end of poetry. Verse
mandate to
plant your arse, diplomacy.

Do. In ya gut
swallow your vowels.
swallow my air
into ya bowels. Let it ream you.
Let ya responses fall
vacuum, a hollow trunk.
Balloon.

Drop ya gut, lush
knit-cast therapeutic knot to
this: you, shame,
unravelling seam,
the hush.

If it improves the silence,
speak. Say only 'shush'.

An Act

Long Title

An Act for the regulation of visiting feet on Country.

1. Name of Act

This Act is the *Binaal Bunma-li, Warra-y Act 2018.*

2. Commencement

This Act is taken to have commenced *yilaalu.*

3. Definitions

Binaal Bunma-li: to soothe or settle down

Warra-y: to get up or swell

Accepted documentary items: such as determined by Elders through Country and prescribed by the regulations.

Regulations: such as determined by Elders through Country.

Feet: gumadhina.

Gumadhina: someone with hardened feet from lots of visiting.

gasp

work work work work work work work work work work work work
work work work work work work work work work work work work
work work work work work *gasp* work work work work work work
work work work work work work work work work work work work
work work work work work work work work work work work work
work work work work work work work work work work work work
work work work work work work work work work work work work
work work work work work work work work work work work work
work work work work work work work work work work work work
work work work work work work work work work work work work
work work work work work work work work work work work work
work work work *gasp* work work work work work work work work
work work work work work work work work work work work work
work work work work *gasp* work work work work work work work
work work work work work work work work work work work work
work work work work work work work work work work work work
work work work work work work work work work work work work
work work work work work work *gasp*. pack pack pack pack pack pack
pack pack pack pack pack pack pack pack pack pack pack pack pack
pack pack pack pack pack pack pack pack pack pack pack pack pack
pack pack pack pack pack pack *gasp* pack pack pack pack pack pack
pack pack pack pack *gasp* run run run run run run run *gasp* run run
run run run run run run run run run run run run run run run run
run run run run run run run run run run run run run run run run
run run run run run run *gasp* run run run run run run run run run run
run run run run run run run run run run run run run run run run
run *gasp*.

gasp.

gasp.

gasp.

work.

the author

Alison Whittaker is a Gomeroi multitasker from the floodplains of Gunnedah. She is a Fulbright scholar, and a poet and essayist whose work has been published in *The Sydney Review of Books*, *Seizure*, *Overland*, *Westerly*, *BuzzFeed*, *Griffith Review*, *The Lifted Brow* and *Meanjin*. In 2015 Alison won the black&write! fellowship for *Lemons in the Chicken Wire* and in 2017 she was awarded the Overland Judith Wright Poetry Prize.

acknowledgements

blakwork was written on Gadigal, Wangal, Gomeroi and Wôpanâak lands.

blakwork took root only because of the work of my Gomeroi mob, my family, all my relations, and my partner.

blakwork was edited by Grace Lucas Pennington.